GREAT RIVERS

RIVERS *of*
BRITAIN
and
IRELAND

THE AVON • YORKSHIRE OUSE
TYNE • WYE • FORTH
LIFFEY • LAGAN

Michael Pollard

Evans

Evans Brothers Limited

First published in 2000 by Evans Brothers Limited

Evans Brothers Limited
2a Portman Mansions
Chiltern Street
London W1U 6NR

© Evans Brothers Limited 2000
First published in paperback in 2002

Commissioned by: Su Swallow
Consultant: Stephen Watts
Series design: Neil Sayer
Book design: Roger Kohn Designs
Editor: Debbie Fox
Picture research: Victoria Brooker
Maps and diagrams: Hardlines

British Library Cataloguing in Publication Data.

Pollard, Michael, 1931 –
    More rivers of Britain. – (Great rivers of Britain)
    1.Rivers – Great Britain – Juvenile literature
    2.Great Britain – History – Juvenile literature
    I.Title
    914.1

ISBN 0237524821

Printed in Hong Kong by Wing King Tong

ACKNOWLEDGEMENTS

For permission to reproduce copyright material, the author
and publishers gratefully acknowledge the following:

Cover (centre) Ecoscene/Farmar (left) Collections/Liz Stares (right) Hans Reinhard/Bruce Coleman Limited **page 3** Mark A Leman/Tony Stone Images **page 6** Collections/Keith Pritchard **page 7** Adam Woolfitt/Robert Harding Picture Library **page 8** Victoria Art Gallery, Bath and North East Somerset Council/Bridgeman Art Library **page 9** Photograph courtesy of Bath & North East Somerset Council **page 10** Skyscan Photolibrary/Pitkin Unichrome Ltd **page 11** (top) Hans Reinhard/Bruce Coleman Limited (bottom) National Trust Photographic Library/David Noton **page 12** Paul Hadley/Robert Harding Picture Library **page 13** (top) Collections/Gary Smith (bottom) B. O'Connor/Robert Harding Picture Library **page 14** Simon Harris/Robert Harding Picture Library **page 15** (middle) Travel Ink/Robert Booth (bottom) Trip/P Terry **page 16** Travel Ink/Ronald Badkin NS160H NYA **page 17** (top) M.R.P Photography (bottom) Collections/Roger Scruton SY-1C-1 **page 18** Trip/M Thornton 10259491 **page 19** (top) The Skyscan Photolibrary T0543 A4 (bottom) Collections/Graeme Peacock GP/39N5B/1 **page 20** Institute of Mechanical Engineers, London/Bridgeman Art Library BAL 5735 **page 21** (top) ASAP/Hulton Deutsch 12945859 (bottom) Vickers Defence Systems **page 22** With thanks to Nissan **page 23** (top) Leslie Garland Picture Library 164.01.09 (bottom)Travel Ink/Leslie Garland QH198L NTB **page 24** Collections/Gena Davies GD/15B/5 **page 25** Trip/Graham Pritchard 10259421 **page 26** Collections/Brian Shuel C-51A-21 **page 27** (top) Trip/C Wormald 10259405 (bottom) Collections/Liz Stares UX360 (repeat of cover) **page 28** Joe Cornish/Tony Stone Images BB4721 **page 29** (top) M-SAT Ltd/Science Photo Library E076/166MSA06H (bottom) Ecoscene/Wayne Lawler AVE160/73 **page 30** (top) © Ecoscene/Farmar 019641 (repeat of cover) (bottom) Mark A Leman/Tony Stone Images BB3848 (repeat of p3) **page 31** Hulton Getty 03305384 or 14315554 **page 32** The Edinburgh Photographic Library 3E 381/T/PD **page 33** (top) The Edinburgh Photographic Library 2A01840/0/MF (bottom) The Edinburgh Photographic Library2|A0693/0/MF **page 34** © Copyright PHOTO IMAGES LTD **page 35** (top) © Copyright PHOTO IMAGES LTD (bottom) Jason Hawkes/Tony Stone Images BB3211 **page 36** © Copyright PHOTO IMAGES LTD **page 37** Intel (check credit) **page 38** Travel Ink/David Toase OE391P DILD **page 39** Leslie Garland Picture Library 20170.01.01 **page 40** Collections/Image Ireland/Errol Forbes SEF-IR33L2-1 **page 41** (top) R.S.A, London/ Bridgeman Art Library RSA 101482 (bottom) Collections/ Image Ireland/Anderson McMeekin XAM-IR33WIC-2 **page 42** Short Brothers **page 43** Collections/ Image Ireland/David Barker XDB-IR33C3-6 **page 44** Hulton Getty 13205231

CONTENTS

THE LOWER AVON – A QUIET RIVER

THE LOWER AVON FLOWS FOR 120 KILOMETRES FROM THE COTSWOLD HILLS, CLOSE TO WILTSHIRE'S BORDER WITH GLOUCESTERSHIRE, TO AVONMOUTH NEAR BRISTOL. THERE, IT MEETS THE SEVERN ESTUARY.

THE NAME 'AVON' comes from the old Celtic word for 'river'. The river is called the Lower Avon, or sometimes the Bristol or North Wiltshire Avon, to avoid confusion with several other British rivers with the same name. One of these, the Upper Avon, is not far away and flows into the Severn near Tewkesbury, less than 50 kilometres from the source of the Lower Avon. Another, often called the Hampshire Avon, rises in south Wiltshire and flows southwards to the English Channel.

THE COTSWOLD HILLS

The Cotswolds are a range of limestone hills running north-eastwards from Bath for a distance of about 90 kilometres. In places they are over 300 metres high. On the western side, the hills slope sharply down to the valley and estuary of the Severn, but to the east the land falls more gently. Streams from the hills meet on an east-facing slope west of Malmesbury to form the Lower Avon, which flows round the southern edge of the Cotswolds.

▲ The Kennet and Avon Canal is part of a waterway route linking London and Bristol. It has been restored and is now used by holiday-makers.

▶ An aerial view of the centre of Bath. At the bottom is one of its best-known streets, the Royal Crescent, built in the eighteenth century.

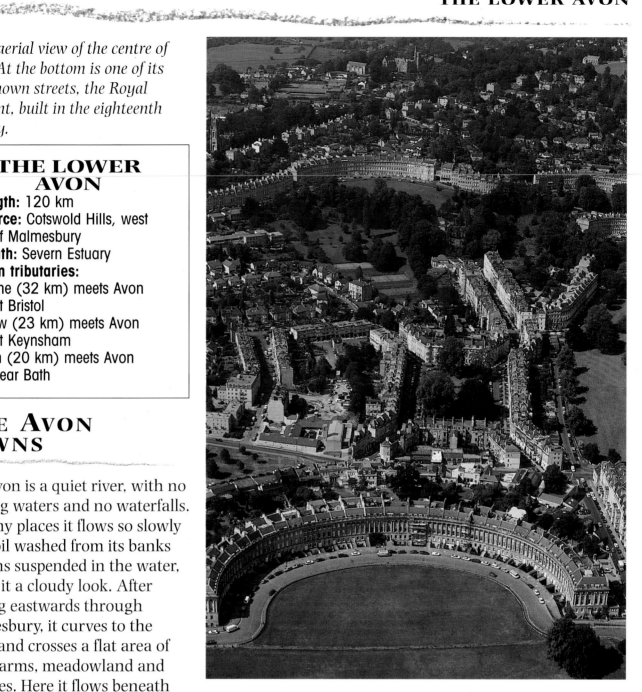

THE LOWER AVON

Length: 120 km
Source: Cotswold Hills, west of Malmesbury
Mouth: Severn Estuary
Main tributaries:
Frome (32 km) meets Avon at Bristol
Chew (23 km) meets Avon at Keynsham
Cam (20 km) meets Avon near Bath

THE AVON TOWNS

The Avon is a quiet river, with no rushing waters and no waterfalls. In many places it flows so slowly that soil washed from its banks remains suspended in the water, giving it a cloudy look. After flowing eastwards through Malmesbury, it curves to the south and crosses a flat area of dairy farms, meadowland and pastures. Here it flows beneath the main east-west rail and road routes linking London with Bristol and South Wales. The Avon passes through Chippenham and Melksham and then reaches Bradford-on-Avon, where the valley sides close in. On the way, it is fed by many small streams from the southern Cotswolds and, to the east, from the chalk downs of northern Wiltshire. From Bradford-on-Avon, a steep-sided valley carries the river on to the city of Bath, which is built in a basin-shaped hollow formed by the river and the surrounding hills. The Kennet and Avon Canal, built in 1794, is also in this valley. It fell into disuse in the 1940s but has now been restored by volunteers. The older houses in Bradford-on-Avon and Bath, and many of the older villages alongside the river, are built of grey stone quarried from the Cotswold Hills.

West of Bath, the Avon crosses another flat area a few kilometres wide before it enters the eastern suburbs of Bristol. After it passes the centre of Bristol, it flows through the Avon Gorge between cliffs up to 75 metres high. Five kilometres further on, the Lower Avon meets the Severn Estuary through the docks at Avonmouth.

WOOL AND WATER

THE TOWNS ALONG THE LOWER AVON SUCH AS CHIPPENHAM, MELKSHAM, BRADFORD-ON-AVON AND BATH WERE IMPORTANT CENTRES OF THE WOOL INDUSTRY FROM THE FOURTEENTH CENTURY UNTIL ABOUT 250 YEARS AGO.

UNTIL THE EARLY 1700s, wool was the most important fibre for making clothes, bedding and carpets. Before wool is spun and woven it has to be washed, and the wool industry grew up in places where there was a good supply of soft, pure water.

WEALTH FROM WOOL

The supply of raw wool for the Wiltshire looms came from huge flocks of sheep on the Cotswold Hills and Salisbury Plain. It was washed in the Avon and spun and woven by hand in the cottages of the small Avon towns. West Country wool was in great demand all over northern Europe, and traders in woollen cloth made huge fortunes. The large houses and churches still to be seen in the Avon towns show how wealthy the woollen industry was.

By about 1740 the industry began to fade away. Cotton from North America began to be used more for

▶ *The Pump Room, Bath, painted soon after it was built in the eighteenth century. It became a meeting-place for rich and fashionable people who came to 'take the waters' at Bath as a cure for a variety of illnesses.*

clothing, while wool manufacture moved to the north of England. There, faster-flowing streams could provide power for weaving as well as water for washing the wool. The towns of the Avon had to look for new ways of earning their living.

TAKING THE WATERS

Bath was to become successful and popular. The Romans knew about the hot springs that flow from the rocks below Bath, and about AD 45 they built a city there which they called *Aquae Sulis* (the waters of Sulis, the Celtic goddess of the springs). Most of the Roman buildings were forgotten until, in the eighteenth century, the baths were

◄ *The Romans built the original baths at Bath almost 2000 years ago. In Roman times they were used not only for bathing but also as a place of worship.*

THE HOT SPRINGS AT BATH

Some of the rain that falls on earth drains away from the surface. The rain that fell on the permeable limestone rock of the Mendip Hills 10,000 years ago seeped through the rock into the earth's crust, to a depth of 4 kilometres. When the water met the impermeable clay it started to collect. As more rain seeps through the limestone, the water table rises. The hot volcanic rocks deep in the earth's crust heat the water to a temperature of up to 90°C. The water is pushed to the surface. It starts to find gaps in the limestone and emerges as hot springs.

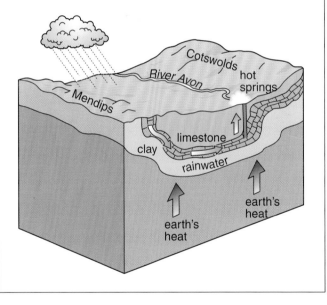

rediscovered. This was the start of a new life for Bath as a fashionable spa where rich families went to bathe in the spring waters. Sheltered in the Avon valley and surrounded by hills, it was a healthy place to live and visitors were soon followed by permanent residents. Grand houses arranged in crescents, parks and squares were built for them, and Bath became a centre of fashionable life.

In 1844, the Great Western Railway was opened, linking London and Bristol. To find a route through the hills, the builders followed the course of the Avon from Bradford-on-Avon westwards through Bath. This made Bath easy to reach and increased its prosperity. Today, most of the buildings of the eighteenth century still stand, and Bath is an important tourist centre.

In the nineteenth century, Melksham, about 25 kilometres upstream from Bath, also tried to turn itself into a health resort to make up for the loss of its wool trade. Hot springs were discovered in 1816 and baths and a pump-room were built, but the small town could not compete with Bath and the project was a failure. In the twentieth century, Melksham has become an industrial town making car tyres and other rubber products, together with smaller factories making furniture and binding books.

PORT ON THE AVON

THE CENTRE OF BRISTOL, THE LARGEST CITY IN THE WEST OF ENGLAND, IS ABOUT TEN KILOMETRES FROM THE MOUTH OF THE AVON.

◀ *Nearly 150 years old, Clifton Suspension Bridge links the wooded slopes to the west of the Avon Gorge with Bristol city centre.*

make Bristol prosperous until the nineteenth century, when the larger ships being built then could no longer navigate up the Avon. New docks were built at the mouth of the Avon on the shores of the Severn, and the city docks are no longer used for shipping. Today, they provide a pleasant open space in the heart of the city, surrounded by a mixture of modern buildings, a major art gallery and old warehouses that have been converted into restaurants.

THE AVON GORGE

The Avon Gorge, sometimes called Clifton Gorge, is a deep cutting made by the Avon through the hills west of Bristol on its way to the Severn Estuary. Above it, the suburb of Clifton, once a separate town, became a popular place to live in the eighteenth century when hot springs were discovered and a spa and pump room were built. The Clifton Suspension Bridge was opened across the Gorge in 1864. With a span of 214 metres, it was one of the first of its kind. Suspension bridges are hung from two steel cables that pass over towers at each end and are then anchored in the ground on each side. More cables connect the main cables with the bridge platform. Although it was designed over 150 years ago for horse-and-cart traffic, the Clifton Suspension Bridge is still able to carry today's vehicles safely.

THE AVON FLOWS through the centre of Bristol along a narrow valley sheltered by hills on all sides. At the western end of the valley the sides close in to form the Avon Gorge. Today, Bristol has spread to cover the hills, but it was the sheltered area by the river that formed the first settlement about 1000 years ago. The first Bristol traders made their fortunes by exporting wool to Flanders and bringing back wine. By the fifteenth century, Bristol was England's second largest city and the Merchant Adventurers, as the Bristol traders called themselves, were rich enough to finance explorations in the 1480s by John Cabot and later by his son, Sebastian Cabot.

The docks in the city centre continued to

RESTORING THE GORGE

Quarrying stone from the sides of the Avon Gorge has laid its rocks bare in places, and, in the early twentieth century, parts of the cliffs on the eastern side were cut away to make way for a new 'low level' road linking Bristol with the docks at Avonmouth. More recently, the people of Bristol have come to value the sides of the Gorge as a green space on the edge of the city. On the western side, Leigh Woods has been laid out with conservation areas and nature walks, with protected habitats for peregrine falcons and other wildlife. Nearby Ashton Court – the largest green area in the city – is the scene of an annual balloon festival where hot-air ballooning enthusiasts show off their skills.

▲ *Peregrine falcons nest along the sides of the Avon Gorge. After many years of falling numbers, the population is now increasing again. Peregrines are famous for their diving speed, reaching up to 300 kilometres per hour.*

◄ *Leigh Woods, on the Avon Gorge, is looked after by the National Trust as a conservation area for trees, flowers, fungi and wildlife.*

THE YORKSHIRE OUSE – FROM THE PENNINES

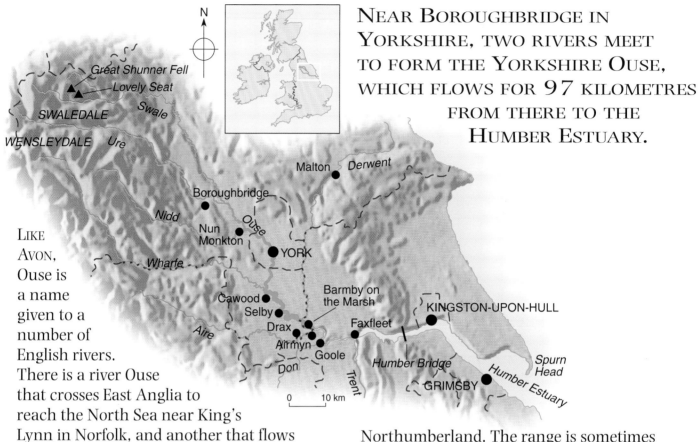

NEAR BOROUGHBRIDGE IN YORKSHIRE, TWO RIVERS MEET TO FORM THE YORKSHIRE OUSE, WHICH FLOWS FOR 97 KILOMETRES FROM THERE TO THE HUMBER ESTUARY.

LIKE AVON, Ouse is a name given to a number of English rivers. There is a river Ouse that crosses East Anglia to reach the North Sea near King's Lynn in Norfolk, and another that flows through East Sussex to the English Channel at Newhaven. The origins of the word 'ouse' are Celtic, meaning 'water'.

PENNINE WATERSHED

The two rivers, the Ure and the Swale, that make up the Yorkshire Ouse start life in the Pennines. The Pennines are a range of high moorland and mountains that runs north and south between north Derbyshire and Northumberland. The range is sometimes called 'the backbone of England'. The Pennines form a boundary between the rivers of England that flow westwards to the Irish Sea and those like the Ure and the Swale that flow eastwards to the North Sea. This kind of boundary is called a watershed. Each side of it, streams and rivers flow in different directions.

The Ure and the Swale start their journeys along two parallel valleys in an area of the northern Pennines called the Yorkshire Dales. The Swale flows down Swaledale and takes its

◀ The Swale near Keld in North Yorkshire. Over centuries, the river has deposited alluvium collected higher up in the mountains, and this provides good pasture-land between the river and the valley sides.

THE YORKSHIRE OUSE

Length: 97 km
Source: Near Boroughbridge
Mouth: Humber Estuary
Main tributaries:

Nidd (56 km) meets Ouse at Nun Monkton

Derwent (92 km) meets Ouse at Barmby on the Marsh

Aire (113 km) meets Ouse at Airmyn

Don (97 km) meets Ouse at Goole

Wharfe (84 km) meets Ouse near Cawood

◄ *Aysgarth Falls on the upper waters of the Ure in Wensleydale. This is one of three cascades that stretch along the river for over two kilometres, during which the water falls 30 metres.*

headwaters from streams flowing down a range of mountains over 600 metres high. The Ure flows down the next valley to the south, which is called Wensleydale. The two valleys are linked by a road, the Buttertubs Pass, which runs high over the mountains between Great Shunner Fell, 713 metres high, and Lovely Seat, 675 metres high. Streams flow from these mountains into both rivers.

Rain and snow fall heavily on the Pennines, turning the mountain streams into rushing torrents. The force of the water tears away fragments of rock and earth which are carried along until the flow slows down and the fragments, called sediment, sink to the river beds. Further action of the water grinds the sediment into silt – fine mud which is carried downstream. This process, over many thousands of years, has created the rich farming country of the Vale of York. Millions of years ago, the Vale was a lake which gradually filled with silt and drained away.

THE HUMBER ESTUARY

On their journey, the Ure and the Swale are joined by many tributaries that also take their water from the Pennines. After each has travelled for about 100 kilometres, they meet and continue almost as far south-eastwards as the Yorkshire Ouse. At the port of Goole, the river begins to widen and flow more slowly, depositing more silt. The mouth of the Ouse continues widening to form the Humber Estuary at Faxfleet, where the Trent joins it from the south. From there, the combined waters of the Ouse and the Trent have another 60 kilometres to travel, under the Humber Bridge and past Hull and Grimsby, before they reach the North Sea at Spurn Head.

◄ *On the hills above the Ure and the Swale, the fields are divided by dry-stone walls built without using cement or mortar.*

13

HISTORIC CITY

THE LARGEST AND MOST IMPORTANT
SETTLEMENT ON THE YORKSHIRE OUSE IS YORK,
WITH A POPULATION OF OVER 176,000.

◀ *The cathedral of St Peter, better known as York Minster, is on the site of a wooden church built in the seventh century. The oldest parts of the present building date from about 1070.*

Northumbria was defeated by Viking invaders who had settled in the area north of the Humber Estuary. When the Normans came in 1066, they conquered York and built a castle there, but it was captured by local rebels. In revenge, William the Conqueror ordered the town to be destroyed.

Today, York is one of the most popular destinations for tourists, with around four million visitors each year. Tourism has become the city's main industry. York's most famous building is the Minster. Parts of the present building date back to Norman times, but there had been a church on the site for about 600 years before that. The Normans also built a wall round the city along which people can still walk.

YORK IS BUILT on a ridge above the flood plain of the Ouse. When the glaciers melted at the end of the last Ice Age about 10,000 years ago, they left behind rocks that they had been carrying with them. The deposit of rocks is known as moraine. The ridge on which York stands is well above the flood level of the Ouse. Until about 200 years ago, before the river was widened south of York, tides from the North Sea came up the Ouse as far as the city.

THE INVADERS CAME

York is a city with a long history. The Roman invaders called it Eboracum and made it their main army headquarters in Britain. After the Romans left, York became the capital of the old kingdom of Northumbria. In AD 865

HOW THE VIKINGS LIVED

Another big tourist attraction in York is the Jorvik Viking Centre, opened in 1984. Jorvik was the Viking name for York. The centre features a reconstruction of the Viking settlement as it was in the tenth century, together with the sounds and smells of that

era. The emphasis is on getting everything exactly right. For example, pictures of Vikings usually show them with horned helmets, but there are no such helmets at the Jorvik Centre because there is no evidence that the Vikings really wore them.

One of York's oldest industries is the manufacture of sweets and chocolate. The Rowntree family set up a factory to make cocoa and chocolate in the nineteenth century. Rowntree's was one of several local firms in the confectionery business, including Craven's who introduced sugared almonds from France. Over the next 100 years Rowntree's began making many popular brands of sweets and chocolate, including Black Magic, Kitcat, Yorkie and Polo mints. Today, the Rowntree factory is owned by the giant international food company Nestlé, based in Switzerland.

◀ *An annual Viking Festival reminds York and its visitors of the 200 years when the city was the capital of a Viking kingdom.*

▶ *Embank-ments along the Ouse prevent flooding as the river flows through York. The Lendal Bridge, in the background, links the two halves of the city and was opened in 1863.*

THE OUSE PLAIN

As you can see from the length of the Yorkshire Ouse's tributaries, water pours into it from a huge area.

THE CATCHMENT AREA of the Ouse and its tributaries stretches from the Tees in the north to the Trent in the south, a distance of almost 100 kilometres, and westwards to the Pennines. The Yorkshire Dales, where the Swale, the Ure and the Wharfe have their sources, are among the wettest parts of Britain. They have an average of over 1500 millimetres of rain each year compared with less than half that figure in eastern England. Other tributaries carry down water from the Cleveland Hills and the North York Moors.

FLOODS

The Vale of York is like a large bowl into which water flows in the autumn, winter and spring. The flow of water is so great that river embankments, flood barriers and networks of drainage channels and dykes are needed to channel water downstream and prevent it from overflowing. Sometimes, heavy rainfall produces more water than the flood defences can cope with, as happened on the Derwent, the Ouse tributary, early in 1999 when homes in the North Yorkshire town of Malton were flooded to a depth of up to three metres. Some

▲ *Canoeists on the river Swale at Grinton in the Yorkshire Dales National Park. The Park provides outdoor activities for thousands of visitors each year.*

people in Selby, on the Ouse, still talk about the spring of 1947 when the snows of a cold winter melted in the hills and flooded their houses to bedroom level. Farmers alongside the Ouse know that unless they keep their drainage ditches clear and flowing, and sometimes dig land drains to take more water off the fields, their fertile soil could quickly turn into a waterlogged wilderness no good for any kind of crop.

THE SELBY COALFIELD

Most of the industry of the Ouse is based on farming. At Selby, for example, there are flour mills, an animal feedstuffs factory, a bacon-curing factory and factories making pickles and other food products. But to the south of Selby, on the edge of the flat land bordering the mouth of the Ouse, the flat landscape is interrupted by the chimneys and cooling towers of two coal-fired power stations,

Eggborough and Drax. It was to feed coal to these power stations that, in the late 1970s, work was begun on a new coalfield 750 metres below ground round Selby despite local worries about subsidence and flooding. A 'pillar' was left undisturbed below Selby town centre and the 900-year-old Selby Abbey. The mines are highly mechanised, with a continuous service of trains delivering the coal direct to the power stations from the pithead. The Selby coal mines are among the few now surviving in Britain.

▶ *A coal conveyor slices the coal from the coalface at Selby mines. Extracting the coal and delivering it to the power-station customers is completely automated.*

▼ *The scene at Malton on the Derwent in early 1999 when the river burst its banks and flooded parts of the town up to three metres deep. An emergency crew checks for people trapped in their homes.*

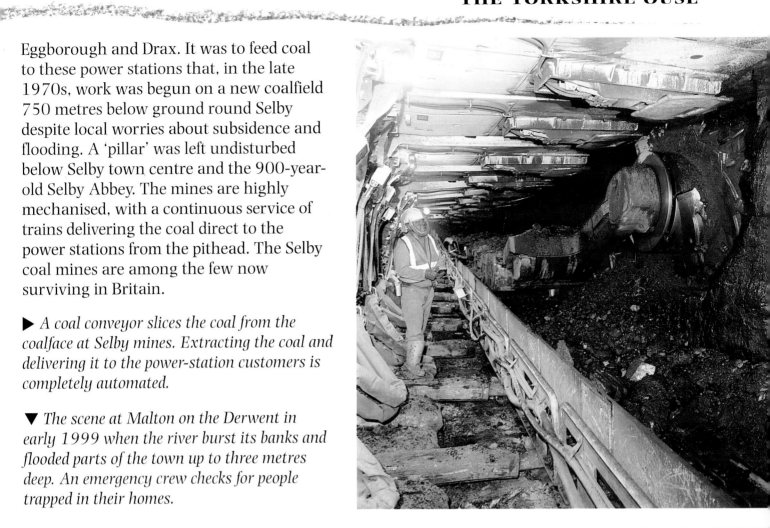

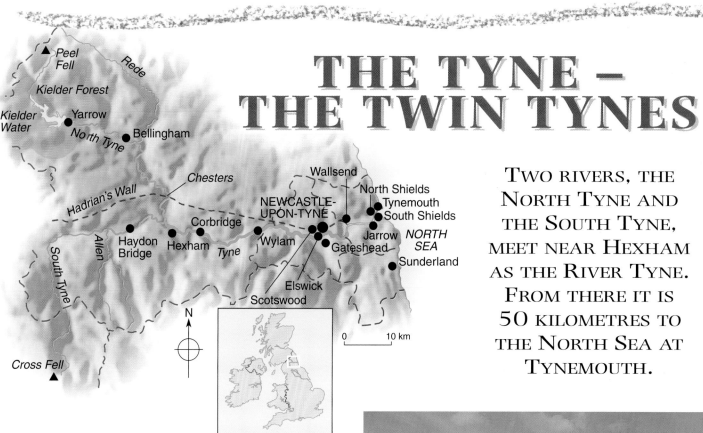

THE TYNE – THE TWIN TYNES

TWO RIVERS, THE NORTH TYNE AND THE SOUTH TYNE, MEET NEAR HEXHAM AS THE RIVER TYNE. FROM THERE IT IS 50 KILOMETRES TO THE NORTH SEA AT TYNEMOUTH.

THE NORTH TYNE rises on Peel Fell, a 602-metre peak of the Cheviot Hills close to the border between England and Scotland. Joined by other mountain streams, it flows for about 12 kilometres until it enters Kielder Water. This is an artificial lake, almost 15 kilometres long, completed in 1983 and designed to provide the water supply for the Teesside area. It is the largest reservoir in Britain. Surrounding it, on what was once heath and moorland, is Kielder Forest, the largest forest in Britain covering 725 square kilometres – about half as large again as the Isle of Man.

MOORLAND AND PASTURE

After leaving Kielder Water through a dam near Yarrow, the North Tyne flows south-eastwards through an area which was once dotted with lead mines. These are now closed, and hill-farming and forestry are the main source of work. As it flows south, the river passes through pastureland. At Chesters near the village of Wall, it is crossed by Hadrian's Wall, the 120-kilometre defensive wall built

▲ As well as storing water for Teesside, Kielder Water provides facilities for a range of watersports including sailing, canoeing, water skiing and sailboarding.

THE TYNE
Length: (from Hexham to Tynemouth) 50 km
Source:
(North Tyne): Peel Fell
(South Tyne): Cross Fell
Mouth: Tynemouth
Main tributaries:
Rede (35 km) meets North Tyne near Bellingham
Allen (23 km) meets South Tyne near Haydon Bridge

◄ *The Roman fort at Chesters where Hadrian's Wall crosses the North Tyne. The barracks at Chesters housed about 500 Roman soldiers.*

Haltwhistle, where it takes a sharp eastward turn and follows the line of Hadrian's Wall a short distance away. Hexham, close to where the rivers meet, grew up round a ferry across the river. The ferry was replaced by a bridge in 1770, but it and its successor were washed away by floods. The present bridge dates from 1793 but was widened in 1967 to deal with increased traffic.

MEETING THE NORTH SEA

Soon after Hexham, the river approaches Tyneside. This is a group of towns, with Newcastle-upon-Tyne at its centre, whose industry was based on coal and iron. The Tyne flows beneath Newcastle's famous six bridges and winds past old industrial sites to the North Sea. There, between piers ending in lighthouses, reaching out from Tynemouth to the north and South Shields to the south, the water that began its journey in the northern Pennines finally reaches the sea.

across northern England by the Romans to protect their northern frontier. A few stones from the Roman bridge can still be seen, together with the foundations of one of the 16 forts situated along the wall. About eight kilometres downstream, near Corbridge, there was another Roman fort – a supply station to the forts that protected a road built by the Romans. The road ran north from York into Scotland and the route it took can still be followed on a modern road map, starting from York as the A19 and then becoming the A68 at Darlington. It ends in Edinburgh.

The sources of the two Tynes are 65 kilometres apart. The South Tyne rises on the slopes of Cross Fell in Cumbria, 893 metres high. It flows north across lonely moorland to

▶ *Two of Newcastle's six bridges across the Tyne. In the foreground is the Swing Bridge, opened in 1876. The George V Bridge, usually known as the Tyne Bridge, was opened in 1929. The Sydney Harbour Bridge in Australia is based on a similar design.*

TYNESIDE INDUSTRY

FROM THE SEVENTEENTH CENTURY, TYNESIDE WAS THE MAIN SUPPLIER OF COAL TO LONDON, SHIPPING IT OUT OF NEWCASTLE AND DOWN THE EAST COAST OF ENGLAND.

IT WAS THE SINKING of deep coal mines, some over 400 metres down, in the early nineteenth century that led to the rise of Tyneside as a centre of heavy industry and engineering. This met the demand for coal as fuel for the iron industry which was growing rapidly. The railways – the great new invention of the time – needed iron for rails, bridges, locomotives and rolling-stock. In the middle of the nineteenth century, iron replaced wood as the building material for ships. Iron was needed, too, for other kinds of new machinery, from threshing machines used to harvest grain on farms to the cranes needed in the shipyards.

RAILWAY PIONEERS

In 1823 George Stephenson, who was born at Wylam on the Tyne and had worked in the mines, opened a factory at Newcastle to make locomotives for the first railways. His son Robert built the Old High Level Bridge over the Tyne at Newcastle, opened in 1849, to carry the England to Scotland railway.

Other Newcastle engineers took advantage of the availability of coal and iron to set up their own enterprises. William George Armstrong founded a business at Elswick in 1846 to make hydraulic machinery. His factory later made heavy guns for the army, and then, when ships made of iron had been

▲ *George Stephenson began his working life looking after horses at a coal mine but soon became fascinated by steam engines. In 1823 he opened a factory in Newcastle to make steam locomotives for the first railways.*

developed, a shipyard was added to the business. Another company, which became Swan Hunter, started making iron ships at Wallsend in 1842 and built many famous vessels. These included the Atlantic liner *Mauretania*, launched in 1907, which held the record for the fastest Atlantic crossing for 20 years.

TURBINE INVENTOR

Another engineer who set up in business in Newcastle was Charles Parsons, who started work at the Armstrong factory in 1877. He was the inventor of the steam turbine, in

◀ A horse-drawn Newcastle coal wagon in 1773. Long before the railway age, wooden tracks were used at collieries to prevent wagons getting bogged down in mud.

which a shaft is driven by the power of steam and forced through the blades of a wheel. In 1889 he set up his own company making turbines to generate electricity, and then he designed a ship driven by steam turbines. He demonstrated his first ship, the *Turbinia*, in 1897, with great success, and went on to set up a works making steam turbines for ships. The *Mauretania* was one of many ocean liners fitted with Parsons engines.

Today, very little of Tyneside's industry is still at work. The Swan Hunter shipyard, the last survivor

of the yards that once lined Tyneside, closed in 1993. Armstrong's Elswick works has closed, although the Vickers company, which took over the business, has a new factory at Scotswood on the banks of the Tyne near Newcastle. As the great days of Tyneside heavy industry become history, the area is exploring new opportunities.

▶ Vickers' Armstrong factory beside the Tyne at Scotswood, where Challenger tanks are built.

TYNESIDE'S TOMORROW

OVER THREE-QUARTERS OF A MILLION PEOPLE LIVE IN
THE TOWNS AND CITIES LINING THE LAST FEW
KILOMETRES OF THE TYNE. NEW DEVELOPMENTS AND
INDUSTRIES HAVE HELPED TO REVITALISE THE AREA.

◀ *Nissan cars lined up for export at the Port of Tyne. Nissan's Sunderland factory is said by experts to be the most efficient car plant in Europe.*

THE DECLINE OF HEAVY INDUSTRY from the 1960s onwards hit Tyneside hard, and the river was lined with abandoned industrial sites. But a few industries are still left. There are ship repair yards at Wallsend and North Shields, and Vickers still make the Challenger tank and other defence vehicles at Scotswood. Taking advantage of the engineering skills of local people and the closeness of the Port of Tyne for exports, Japanese car-makers Nissan have set up a factory complex in Sunderland employing 4200 people and making over 270,000 cars each year. Developments like this also provide employment in 'spin off' services for many people outside the factory gates, such as suppliers of components and of services such as catering and cleaning.

The Port of Tyne is still busy, with roll-on-roll-off cargo and passenger services to northern Europe, a container terminal, facilities for bulk cargoes and the export of Sunderland-made cars to 58 countries worldwide. But most people at work on Tyneside have found jobs in new fields.

WELCOMING TOURISTS

One new industry is tourism. Ferry services from Norway, Sweden, Germany and Holland make Tyneside a magnet for visitors from northern Europe, and Newcastle in particular has gone out of its way to welcome them. One attraction is the Metro Centre just outside the city, until recently Britain's largest shopping complex. Since 1989, ten major hotels have been built in Newcastle. Other developments include the Newcastle Arena (an exhibition and conference centre and sports venue seating 10,000 and opened in 1995), the Centre for Life (an interactive museum

◀ Newcastle's Quayside market is open on Sundays every week. It is a popular attraction for local residents and visitors alike.

opening on the river in 2000), and a waterside arts centre converted from a former flour mill. The Royal Quays project is a scheme which will provide 1,200 new homes, together with industrial units and offices, planned around a marina and a park with watersports facilities. In the centre of Newcastle three 150-year-old streets known as Grainger Town, which had suffered from shop closures and traffic problems, are being renovated to provide new housing, shops and offices. Other moves to solve traffic problems are the building of a new footbridge across the Tyne, which will swing open to allow ships through, and a new ring road to take traffic round the city instead of through it.

Meanwhile, at Wallsend, there is a dockland conversion at St Peter's Basin that will provide 285 luxury apartments over-looking the Tyne, together with moorings for yachts.

As if to show that all the towns in the Tyneside area must stick together, there are plans to extend Newcastle's highly successful Metro underground system, which already carries 40 million passengers a year, to Sunderland.

▲ Sailing ships visiting Newcastle's Quayside in 1993 for the start of the annual Tall Ships Race. The tall building in the background is the old Baltic Flour Mill, now an arts centre.

THE WYE – A SCENIC RIVER

THE WYE RISES IN WALES, FLOWS INTO THE SEVERN ESTUARY, AND FOR ABOUT 30 KILOMETRES SOUTH OF MONMOUTH FORMS THE BOUNDARY BETWEEN WALES AND ENGLAND.

THE LENGTH OF THE Wye, the river known in Welsh as Afon Gwy, is 210 kilometres. Its source is on the eastern slopes of Plynlimon, 752 metres high in the mountains of central Wales. This is only about five kilometres away from the source of the Severn, which the Wye meets at the end of its course in the Bristol Channel.

ACROSS THE MOUNTAINS

▼ *Waterskiing on the Wye is a popular pastime. The unpolluted water and beautiful scenery attract watersports enthusiasts.*

To many people, the Wye is Britain's most beautiful river. From its source, it flows for 30 kilometres across remote upland country where a single road, heading for the Welsh coast at Aberystwyth from the Midlands and South Wales, follows the river valley. Close by is a series of reservoirs created in the late nineteenth century by flooding the valleys of the rivers Elan and Claerwen, which are tributaries of the Wye. These reservoirs supply water by pipeline to Birmingham, 120 kilometres away.

Passing Rhayader, a small but important village where main roads meet from north, south, east and west, the Wye plunges again through a rocky channel to Builth Wells,

where tributaries flowing in from both sides have created a small plain. Before the days of long distance road and rail transport, Builth Wells was an important stopping-place for cattle drovers driving their flocks to market in England.

THE PLAIN OF HEREFORD

About 20 kilometres downstream from Builth Wells, the Wye, which so far has flowed south-eastwards, makes a sudden turn north-east. This diversion is caused by the Black Mountains, rising to well over 700 metres, which lie in the river's path. The Wye turns into a valley where it is fed by streams from north-facing slopes of the Black Mountains, and near Hay-on-Wye crosses the border into England. The valley opens out into the Plain of Hereford – good cattle-rearing country dominated by Hereford itself, the largest settlement on the river with a population of 50,000. Above and below Hereford, the river sweeps in a series of wide meanders across the flood plain with steep wooded cliffs on the outsides of the curves and more gentle slopes on the insides. Below Ross-on-Wye the Wye flows along the north-western edge of the Forest of Dean, which was once a coal and iron mining area, until it reaches Monmouth and makes its final turn south. At Monmouth the Wye and its tributary the Monnow have formed a small, sheltered basin in which the town grew up. From Monmouth to Chepstow, the Wye flows through a steep-sided wooded valley. This 30-kilometre stretch of the river contains some of the Wye's finest scenery. Finally, below Chepstow, the Wye opens out into mud flats and enters the Severn Estuary under the 1966 Severn Road Bridge.

▼ *Ross-on-Wye, dominated by its church spire, is one of the attractive small towns on the banks of the lower Wye.*

THE WYE
Length: 210 km
Source: Plynlimon, Cambrian Mountains
Mouth: Severn Estuary
Main tributaries:
Elan (22 km) meets Wye near Rhayader
Claerwen (25 km) meets Wye near Rhayader
Ithon (16 km) meets Wye near Builth Wells
Irfon (24 km) meets Wye at Builth Wells
Chwefru (19 km) meets Wye at Builth Wells
Edw (22 km) meets Wye at Aberedw
Lugg (64 km) meets Wye at Mordiford
Monnow (64 km) meets Wye at Monmouth

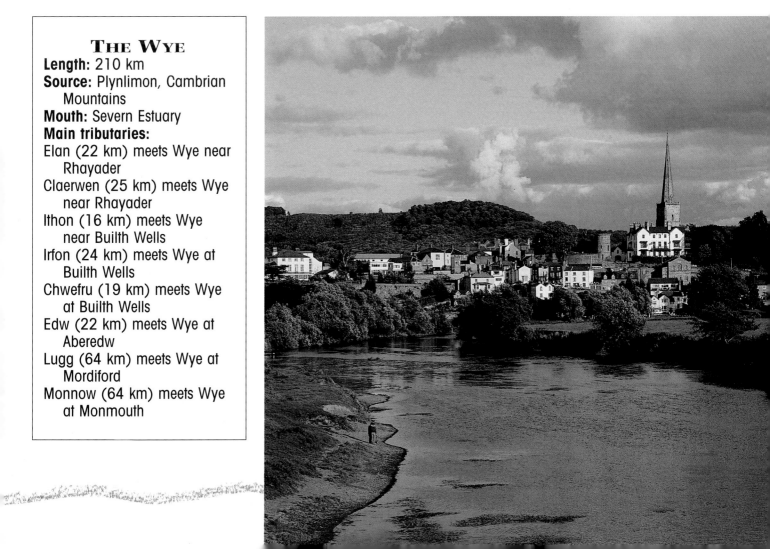

MAGNET FOR VISITORS

AN EXCITING HISTORY, BEAUTIFUL SCENERY AND RIVER SPORTS MAKE THE WYE VALLEY A MAGNET FOR VISITORS FROM ALL OVER BRITAIN AND ABROAD.

THE BORDER BETWEEN England and Wales was a scene of conflict for many hundreds of years. The people of Wales had a reputation for wildness, and in the eighth century AD the king of the Saxon kingdom of Mercia, Offa, built an earthwork to mark the boundary between the two countries. This is called Offa's Dyke. It ran from near Chepstow northwards to the River Clwyd in north Wales. Today, it forms the basis of the 285-kilometre long Offa's Dyke Long Distance Footpath. From Chepstow to Monmouth the Dyke and the footpath run close to the Wye, on the English side of the river. Here, the limestone cliffs form the western edge of the Forest of Dean plateau, and the path running along the top of the cliffs gives breathtaking views of the river below.

BORDER WARS

Offa's Dyke was built to mark the boundary, not as a defence against Welsh invaders. But border wars between the Welsh and English continued through several centuries until Edward I of England finally conquered Wales in 1282. The line of castles such as those at Chepstow, St Briavels, Goodrich near Ross-on-Wye, Hay-on-Wye and Builth Wells – together with many more that are now in ruins or

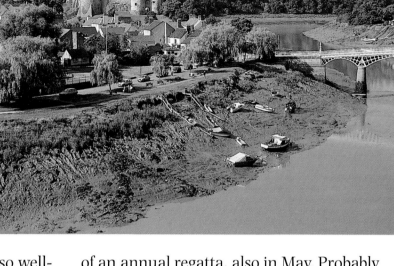

▶ *In a commanding position on the west bank of the Wye, the castle at Chepstow protected the road into South Wales and river traffic.*

have disappeared altogether – is a reminder of those old wars.

The Wye owes its popularity with visitors to the fact that no heavy industry has ever developed along it. As a result, there are no sprawling industrial sites or abandoned factories. It is one of Britain's least polluted rivers and England's best river for salmon. It is also well-used by canoeists who can travel the length of the river and enjoy the thrill of negotiating rapids and 'white water'. One of the highlights of the year is the three-day River Wye Raft Race which takes place between Hay-on-Wye and Chepstow each May. Hereford is the scene

◀ *Swift-running and pollution-free, the Wye is one of Britain's most popular rivers for salmon fishing. As long ago as 1188, a monk described the numbers of salmon in its waters.*

▼ *Rafting is a tradition on the Wye. Rafts were once used to carry cargoes such as timber down the river. Today, rafting is a popular leisure pursuit.*

of an annual regatta, also in May. Probably the best-known tourist spot on the Wye is Symond's Yat between Monmouth and Ross-on-Wye. This is an outcrop of limestone over 150 metres high round which the river winds in a horseshoe bend that is eight kilometres long. The sides of the rock are steep and wooded and are the home of many nests of peregrine falcons and other protected species of birds.

MUSIC AND LITERATURE

For visitors who prefer dry land, the people in charge of tourism in the Wye area have cleverly developed a wide range of activities. Hereford has an annual May Fair and music festival. Hay-on-Wye is an internationally famous centre of the second-hand book trade and also hosts an annual literary festival. The Welsh side of the Wye valley between Monmouth and Chepstow is an almost continuous stretch of forest trails and woodland walks, and on the English side visitors can take the Wye Valley Walk for 82 kilometres from Chepstow north as far as Hereford. For bird-watchers, the mud flats south of Chepstow, where the Wye takes a sharp bend to meet the Severn Estuary, provide constant observation of the comings and goings of migrating species.

THE FORTH – CROSSING SCOTLAND

THE HEADWATERS OF THE FORTH ARE MOUNTAIN STREAMS WHICH RISE OVER 970 METRES HIGH ON THE EASTERN SLOPES OF BEN LOMOND, ABOUT 40 KILOMETRES NORTH-WEST OF GLASGOW IN AN AREA CALLED THE TROSSACHS.

THE HEADWATERS OF THE FORTH are Duchray Water and the Laggan, which collect other streams as they flow eastwards. Near Aberfoyle they come together to form the Forth. From there on the Forth follows a winding course across a wide valley to Stirling. On the way, more streams and small rivers join it from the mountains to the north and south.

THE FORTH

Length: (including the Firth) 183 km
Source: Ben Lomond
Mouth: Firth of Forth
Main tributaries:
Goodie Water (20 km) meets Forth at Blairdrummond Moss
Teith (22 km) meets Forth west of Stirling
Allan (39 km) meets Forth near Bridge of Allan
Devon (39 km) meets Forth at Cambus
Carron (15 km) meets Forth at Grangemouth

THE BATTLES OF THE BRIDGE

The Forth gave Stirling a key place in Scottish history. Until 1936 it was the first point from the east where the river could be crossed by road. For 500 years, from the thirteenth century to the eighteenth, there was a series of wars between the English and the Scots. The

▶ *The present-day castle at Stirling was mostly built between 400 and 500 years ago, but there has been a castle on the site for well over 1000 years.*

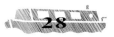

▲ *This true colour photograph taken from a Landsat satellite shows the Forth-Clyde valley and the Firth of Forth. The grey areas are settlements. Glasgow is at the bottom left and Edinburgh is the grey area to the south of the Firth.*

Forth, with its bridge at Stirling, was a huge obstacle for English armies marching north. A volcanic rock rises over 120 metres above the low-lying and marshy ground beside the river, commanding a view in all directions and with sheer cliff-faces on two sides. It was the perfect site for a fort, and from the twelfth to the seventeenth century Stirling Castle was the headquarters and palace of the Scottish kings.

The land below the castle was the scene of two famous battles in Scottish history. In 1297 Scotland's great national hero William Wallace soundly defeated an invading English army at the Battle of Stirling Bridge, catching the soldiers at a disadvantage when they were half-way across. In 1314 another famous Scots leader, Robert the Bruce, led his army to victory over the English at the Battle of Bannockburn, four kilometres away on the Forth flood plain. Today, Stirling Castle attracts thousands of visitors each year as an example of a fortress with hundreds of years of history.

THE FIRTH OF FORTH

Below Stirling, the Forth continues to wind through an area known as the 'Links of Forth' as far as Alloa, where it begins to open out into the Firth of Forth. From its start near Aberfoyle to Kincardine Bridge, near Alloa,

the course of the Forth is 106 kilometres long, although the distance in a direct line is only 48 kilometres. Its water still has to travel another 77 kilometres down the Firth before it reaches the North Sea. In this distance it widens from less than one kilometre at Kincardine to over 28 kilometres.

The word 'firth' is used in Scotland to describe an inlet of the sea which is the mouth of a river. These inlets were formed about 10,000 years ago, when the last Ice Age ended and the glaciers began to melt. The melting ice gouged out deep channels in the earth's surface. When the ice finally reached the sea and melted completely, it raised the level of the sea, which flowed inland to flood the channels. Other Scottish flooded river valleys include the Moray Firth, the Dornoch Firth, the Firth of Cromarty and the Firth of Clyde.

▲ *Bass Rock, standing 107 metres above the sea, marks the southern entrance to the Firth of Forth. In the seventeenth century a fort on the rock, now demolished, was used as a prison. Today, the only inhabitants are thousands of seabirds.*

BRIDGING THE FORTH

◀ *The two Forth Bridges. On the left is the road bridge, opened in 1964, with its twin towers carrying cables supporting the deck. The rail bridge on the right was opened in 1890.*

FOR MANY HUNDREDS OF YEARS, THE FIRTH OF FORTH WAS A BARRIER TO TRAVEL TO THE HIGHLANDS OF SCOTLAND AND TO THE NORTHERN CITIES OF PERTH, DUNDEE, ABERDEEN AND INVERNESS.

THE MAIN TRAFFIC on Scottish roads until the late nineteenth century was the cattle brought south by drovers to be sold in the great market at Falkirk. The drovers crossed the Forth at Stirling, where they watered the cattle in the river before the last stage of the journey to Falkirk, about 20 kilometres further on. The first railway north of Stirling also crossed the Forth there. This railway brought an end to droving, because it was cheaper to load cattle on to trains than to drive them south on foot.

▶ *The rail bridge at sunset, with the road bridge in the background. It was once a tradition that rail passengers crossing the bridge threw pennies into the water, but modern coaches with sealed windows have ended the custom.*

WONDER OF THE WORLD

The first bridge lower down the Forth was opened in 1890, and carried the railway line from Edinburgh northwards to Inverness. It is a cantilever bridge with two central spans, using the small island of Inch Garvie in the

◀ *The Forth Rail Bridge under construction in the 1880s. It took seven years to build, and provided jobs for a workforce of over 5000.*

Forth Road Bridge was opened close to the Rail Bridge at Queensferry. This is a suspension bridge, 1876 metres long, with the cables that support the deck suspended from two tall towers built on the bed of the Forth. Today, the Forth Road Bridge is at the southern end of a motorway system that takes traffic to Perth, Aberdeen and the Highlands. On the south side of the river, it joins up with motorways linking Edinburgh, Stirling and Glasgow.

middle of the Firth as a stepping-stone. At the time it seemed a wonder of engineering, and it was then the longest cantilever bridge in the world. Each of the two central spans is 521 metres long and built of steel tubes up to four metres in diameter. The total length of the bridge from bank to bank is 2526 kilometres.

CROSSING BY ROAD

The Forth Rail Bridge made direct rail travel to the north of Scotland possible, but road traffic still had to travel north through Stirling until 1936. Then the Kincardine Bridge, near Grangemouth, was opened, providing a more direct route to northern Scotland from Edinburgh and also from Glasgow. By the time the Kincardine Bridge was opened there was already too much traffic at peak times for it to carry. But it was not until 1964 that a new

By the 1990s the amount of traffic crossing the Forth had increased beyond the capacity of the two bridges. The Kincardine Bridge alone was carrying 25,000 vehicles a day. Three sites were suggested for a third bridge, and in November 1998, after long discussions with conservationists and local people, the site was finally chosen. It will be two kilometres upstream (west) from the present Kincardine Bridge, and each bridge will then carry traffic in only one direction. Work is expected to start on the new bridge in 2003.

CHANGES ON THE FORTH

THE FIRTH OF FORTH HAS BEEN A CENTRE OF SCOTTISH INDUSTRY FOR OVER 250 YEARS.

▼ *The giant oil and petrochemicals plant at Grangemouth where crude oil is refined to produce petrol and chemical by-products.*

THERE WERE COALFIELDS and iron-ore mines in Fife to the north and Lothian to the south. For 150 years, the giant Carron ironworks near Falkirk was the largest single industrial plant in the east of Scotland. Leith, Grangemouth, Methil, Burntisland, Kirkcaldy and Granton were all busy ports and industrial towns on the Firth of Forth.

THE FORTH PORTS

Most of the old industries of the Firth of Forth, such as iron-making, coal-mining and shipbuilding, have gone. But, since the discovery of North Sea oil in the 1960s, Grangemouth and Mossmoran in Fife have become important centres for oil and

◀ *The former Royal Yacht* Britannia, *now moored at Leith. Launched in 1953, the year of Queen Elizabeth II's coronation, it served the royal family for 44 years and sailed over 1,500,000 kilometres.*

petrochemicals. Petrochemicals are loaded at Grangemouth docks and oil is exported through a specially-built terminal at Hound Point, opened in 1975. There is a second oil terminal at Braefoot Bay.

Leith is still a working port, but many of its waterfront buildings have found new uses as restaurants and wine bars. One of Leith's most popular new attractions is Waterworld, which offers more than 20 water features such as chutes and bubble pools. Since 1998 Leith has been the home of the former Royal Yacht *Britannia*, retired in 1997 after over 40 years of royal duties. A new Ocean Terminal for ocean-going yachts will open in 2000, and *Britannia* will be its main feature.

The south bank of the Forth is dominated by Edinburgh, Scotland's capital city since 1437 and now the site of the new Scottish Parliament. The 'Old Town' of Edinburgh was built on extinct volcanoes and rocky outcrops facing north over the Firth of Forth. In the eighteenth century the city expanded with the building of the elegant squares and broad streets of the 'New Town'. Since then, the city has spread along the south bank of the Forth to take in places like Leith and Newhaven, which were once separate settlements.

The new developments in Leith are part of Edinburgh's efforts to boost its tourist industry. In 1947 the city began the Edinburgh International Festival of Music

and Drama, now the largest of its kind in the world attracting about one million visitors in August and September each year. The aim now is to attract large numbers of visitors through the rest of the year. There is a fine collection of museums and art galleries that has been added to with the opening in 1998 of a large extension to the Royal Museum of Scotland and in 1999 of the William Younger Centre, an interactive exhibition of earth's history.

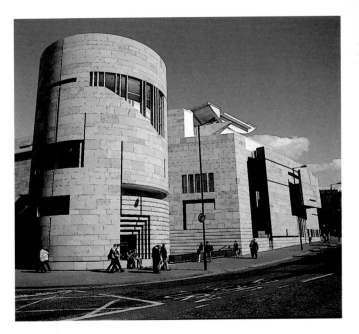

▲ *The new extension to the Museum of Scotland, opened in 1998 and described as 'Edinburgh's most stunning piece of modern architecture'. The roof offers visitors a panoramic view of the city.*

THE LIFFEY – FROM THE WICKLOW MOUNTAINS

THE LIFFEY — KNOWN TO IRISH-SPEAKERS AS AN LIFE — FLOWS FOR 80 KILOMETRES FROM THE NORTHERN WICKLOW MOUNTAINS TO DUBLIN BAY.

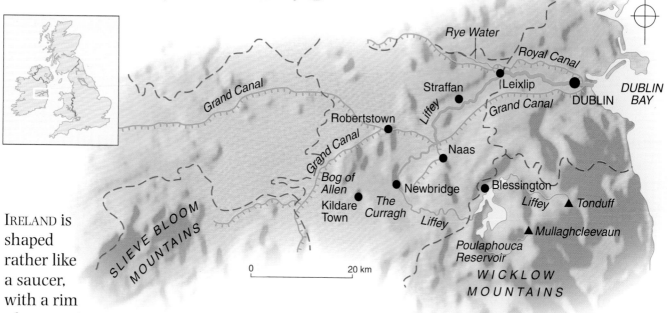

Rye Water · Royal Canal · Grand Canal · Straffan · Leixlip · DUBLIN · DUBLIN BAY · Liffey · Grand Canal · Robertstown · Naas · Grand Canal · Bog of Allen · Newbridge · Blessington · Kildare Town · The Curragh · Liffey · Liffey · Tonduff · Mullaghcleevaun · Poulaphouca Reservoir · SLIEVE BLOOM MOUNTAINS · WICKLOW MOUNTAINS

0   20 km

N

IRELAND is shaped rather like a saucer, with a rim of mountains surrounding a central plain. In the last Ice Age, 10,000 years ago, the whole of the British Isles except for southern England was covered with ice sheets. When these retreated, the melted water formed the Irish Sea and cut off Ireland from England. At the same time, the ice left behind a deposit of limestone and clay in Ireland's central plain.

The valley of the lower Liffey runs south-west from Dublin to give access to the central plain from Ireland's major city. To the east are the Wicklow Mountains. To the west is the Bog of Allen, a large area of peat bog (see page 35), which is at least 5000 years old. To the south-west are the Slieve Bloom Mountains, rising to over 500 metres.

The source of the Liffey is on Tonduff, at 642 metres one of the highest mountains in the Wicklow range south of Dublin. The Wicklows are granite mountains, divided by deep glens. The mountains are part of the line of granite

◀ *An aerial view of the Bog of Allen. The scars show where the peat has been cut for use as fuel or by gardeners.*

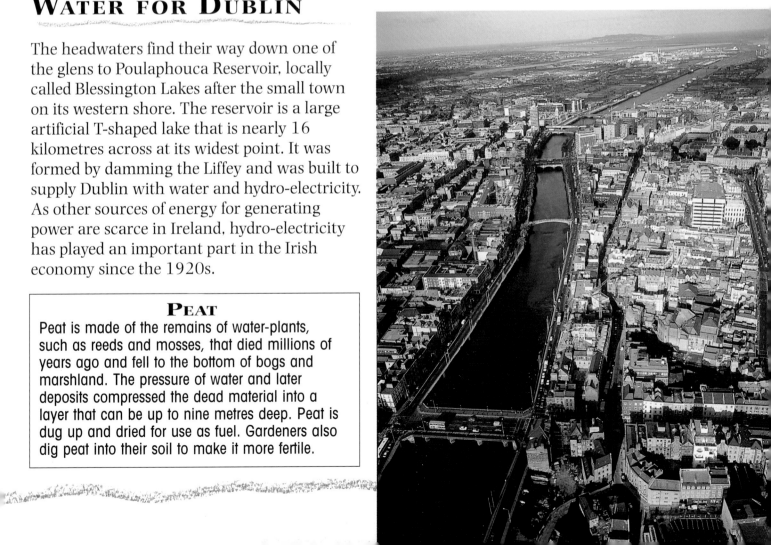

THE LIFFEY
Length: 80 km
Source: Tonduff,
  Wicklow Mountains
Mouth: Dublin Bay

▶ *The dam at the head of Poulaphouca Reservoir, through which water flows to drive turbines and generate electricity.*

which runs from the south-west to the north-east of the British Isles, reappearing in England's Lake District.

WICKLOW'S REBELS

In the eighteenth century the deep glens were the strongholds of rebels who resisted the British occupation of Ireland and occasionally came down from the mountains to raid the villages in the Liffey valley. In 1798 the British Army built a Military Road across the Wicklow Mountains, with guardhouses at intervals, in an attempt to subdue the rebels. The road, which today is popular with walkers, passes close to the source of the Liffey.

WATER FOR DUBLIN

The headwaters find their way down one of the glens to Poulaphouca Reservoir, locally called Blessington Lakes after the small town on its western shore. The reservoir is a large artificial T-shaped lake that is nearly 16 kilometres across at its widest point. It was formed by damming the Liffey and was built to supply Dublin with water and hydro-electricity. As other sources of energy for generating power are scarce in Ireland, hydro-electricity has played an important part in the Irish economy since the 1920s.

PEAT
Peat is made of the remains of water-plants, such as reeds and mosses, that died millions of years ago and fell to the bottom of bogs and marshland. The pressure of water and later deposits compressed the dead material into a layer that can be up to nine metres deep. Peat is dug up and dried for use as fuel. Gardeners also dig peat into their soil to make it more fertile.

The Liffey leaves the reservoir at its south-western end, heading west at first and then turning north to run along the edge of the central plain through farming country and small villages. It enters Dublin from the south-west and then turns sharply to flow through the city centre, ending its journey to the Irish Sea in Dublin Bay.

▼ *The Liffey divides north and south Dublin but road, rail and pedestrian bridges link the two halves of the city.*

THE LIFFEY VALLEY

THE LIFFEY VALLEY CONTAINS EVIDENCE OF
IRELAND'S OLD WAY OF LIFE AS WELL AS
SIGNS OF THE COUNTRY'S NEW GROWTH
AND DEVELOPMENT.

THE LIFFEY VALLEY carries the main roads and railways from Dublin to the south and west. The Liffey also provided the route and the water supply for the canal system built in the middle of the eighteenth century to connect Dublin with southern and western Ireland. In those days, Irish roads were so bad that the safest and fastest way to travel was by barge, and the canals carried large numbers of passengers as well as cargo. They are no longer used for trade, but in some places there are tourist cruises along them. The Grand Canal follows the course of the Liffey from Dublin to near Naas, where it then heads towards the River Shannon on the west coast. A short branch connects the Grand Canal with Naas itself, and another branch runs south from Robertstown to link up with the River Barrow and the port of Waterford. The Royal Canal heads west from Dublin towards County Westmeath.

IRELAND'S FAVOURITE SPORT

The area around Naas and Newbridge (sometimes still known by its Irish name Droichead Nua) is the centre of Ireland's prosperous horse-racing industry. Close to Newbridge is the Curragh, a fertile plain formed during the last Ice Age when the meltwater from retreating ice sheets ground the limestone rock to a fine powder. The Curragh racecourse is the headquarters of Irish racing, where the Irish Derby and other classic races are run. There are also racecourses at Naas and Punchestown, and not far away, near Kildare Town, is the Irish National Stud, devoted to breeding champion racehorses, and the National Stud Horse Museum.

Horse-racing is part of Irish sporting culture, but it is rivalled today by golf. Ireland

▶ *Racing at the Curragh. The word means 'racecourse' in the Irish language, and it is said that races have been held there for nearly 2000 years.*

has spent nearly £250 million in the 1990s on new and re-designed golf courses, mainly for their tourist appeal. There are now over 330. One of the newest is the K Club on the banks of the Liffey at Straffan, about 25 kilometres from Dublin. It was designed by the American golfer Arnold Palmer, four times winner of the US Masters Championship, in the 1960s.

NEW INDUSTRY

The towns of the Liffey valley also show examples of Ireland's industrial development. Leixlip, where there are waterfalls on the Liffey now used to generate hydro-electricity, is one of Ireland's success stories. The Intel Corporation, the world's largest makers of microchips, opened a factory there in 1989 to make what were then the new Pentium chips. There are now three factories on the site, employing more than 4000 people. Leixlip has become Intel's European centre for manufacturing microchips and researching new developments in the microchip industry. The third generation of Pentium chips, Pentium III, went into production in 1999.

DUBLIN, CITY OF CHANGE

THE CITY OF DUBLIN HAS A POPULATION OF ALMOST 480,000, BUT ABOUT HALF OF THE IRISH REPUBLIC'S POPULATION OF 3.5 MILLION LIVE IN THE DUBLIN AREA.

◀ *Newly pedestrianised and tidied up, Temple Bar on the south side of the Liffey has become the centre of Dublin's cultural and night life, especially for the city's young people.*

DUBLIN'S OLD CITY CENTRE was created in a period of about 30 years in the eighteenth century in the Georgian style – a style named after the British kings of the time. The buildings include Trinity College – Ireland's leading university – and the elegant Merrion and Fitzwilliam Squares.

By the 1970s Dublin suffered from an industrial decline. Things changed soon after Ireland joined the European Union in 1973. It was then one of the poorest European countries and was given large grants to improve the quality of life and develop trade and industry. Some of this money was spent on modernising Irish farming, but some was also invested in the cities, including Dublin.

FLOCKING TO DUBLIN

The result of the EC grants was a massive building programme that is still going on. Multinational corporations, especially those involved in telecommunications, service industries and computer software, were attracted to the city and brought with them large numbers of young professional people from America, Japan, northern Europe and the Middle East. A city in decline has been revitalised.

New building is going on everywhere. On the north bank of the Liffey, the old Custom House Quay has been transformed into a modern development which includes an international financial services centre. On the

south side, the Temple Bar area, which was run down and at one time was threatened with being turned into a huge car park, has been developed as a pedestrianised district of new apartments, art galleries, shops, cafes, music venues, arts centres and a hotel. There have been conversions as well as new buildings. Dublin's tourist office is housed in a former church and Powerscourt House, built in 1771, has become the centrepiece of a new shopping precinct. Dublin's contribution to the new Millennium is an illuminated spire, 120 metres tall, which will be built in the city's most famous street, O'Connell Street.

▼ *The Ha'penny Bridge links Temple Bar with the north bank of the Liffey. It was given its name because for many years pedestrians were charged a toll of half an old penny (about 0.2p) to use it.*

WORLD-FAMOUS

Alongside all this activity, there has been a boom in Irish cultural exports. Groups such as U2, the Boomtown Rats, the Corrs and Boyzone and singers like Christy Moore and Sinead O'Connor – who all began their careers in Dublin – have become part of the international pop music scene and are recognised all over the world. More recently, in 1994, the dance company Riverdance, booked to fill in an interval in the Eurovision Song Contest, exploded on to the international scene. These successes have put Dublin on the world map and made it a truly international city. One of the best results, from the Irish point of view, is that an increasing number of young Irish people who come to Dublin as students stay on to work there instead of emigrating to North America or Great Britain.

THE LAGAN – BELFAST'S RIVER

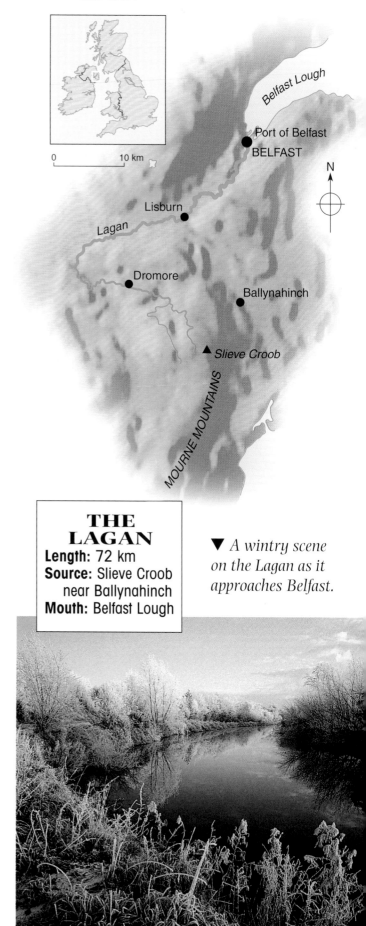

THE LAGAN STARTS ITS JOURNEY TO THE IRISH SEA ON SLIEVE CROOB, A 532-METRE HIGH NORTHERN OUTCROP OF THE MOURNE MOUNTAINS SOUTH OF BELFAST.

LEAVING THE MOUNTAINS, the Lagan flows first west and then north-east through rich pastureland. This part of Ireland is protected from the south-west winds by mountains and so has less rain than the rest of the country. The flood plain has built up over thousands of years from sediment brought down from the mountains by the river, making alluvial soil rich in plant nutrients. The fields beside the Lagan are used to fatten cattle for market.

THE FLOOD PLAIN

A number of small towns are dotted along the banks of the river across the flood plain. Many of them had linen mills, using flax grown on the flood plain, and the open spaces beside the river were used to spread out the finished cloth to bleach it in the sun. Many Irish towns are very small, but Dromore on the Lagan has a population of about 4000. The town was once more important than it is today. An abbey was founded there in the sixth century, and it later became a cathedral. But in 1641 there was civil war in Ireland and almost every building in the town was destroyed in the fighting. The present cathedral was built in 1661. Today, the main Belfast to Dublin

THE LAGAN
Length: 72 km
Source: Slieve Croob near Ballynahinch
Mouth: Belfast Lough

▼ *A wintry scene on the Lagan as it approaches Belfast.*

◄ *An old print showing an Irish linen mill. The strips of finished cloth are laid out to be bleached in the sun.*

Lagan valley were planted with flax, the plant which gives the fibre from which linen is made. Lisburn had the water of the Lagan to power its mills, land along the banks of the river to bleach its linen fabric, and the port of Belfast nearby through which finished linen could be exported all over the world. The industry was started by Huguenots who came from France and the Netherlands as refugees from religious persecution in the eighteenth century. The linen industry survives today, but on a far smaller scale, making expensive heavy damask for luxury furnishings and designer fabric for the fashion trade. Lisburn is an important tourist centre, and in 1999 the Lagan Valley LeisurePlex, a new centre for watersports, was opened, with swimming pools, water rides and spa pools.

road crosses the Lagan at Dromore.

Soon afterwards the Lagan takes a wide curve to the north-west and reaches Lisburn, 13 kilometres south of Belfast.

LINEN CITY

Lisburn was the heart of Northern Ireland's linen industry for 200 years, and this is remembered today in the city's Irish Linen Centre. In the nineteenth century, about 100 square kilometres of land in and around the

► *Belfast's Waterfront Centre beside the Lagan has put Belfast on the international music scene.*

NORTHERN IRELAND'S CAPITAL

THE LAGAN FLOWS THROUGH BELFAST INTO
BELFAST LOUGH, AN INLET OF THE IRISH SEA
ABOUT 24 KILOMETRES LONG.

▲ *Sunderland flying-boats moored next to the Harland and Wolff shipyard during the Second World War.*

▶ *These engineers at Shorts are working on the fuselage of a Learjet 45.*

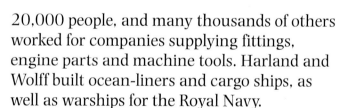

BELFAST, sheltered at the southern end of Belfast Lough, began as a walled fishing village with a ferry across the Lagan. It was turned into a city by the Industrial Revolution of the early nineteenth century. First came the development of Belfast as a port, mainly to serve the linen industry. Shipbuilding began in 1791, and 1861 saw the founding of the Harland and Wolff yard.

MAJOR SHIPBUILDERS

Harland and Wolff was to dominate Belfast shipbuilding, building and equipping ships to meet an ever-growing demand. At its peak in the 1920s, the company employed over 20,000 people, and many thousands of others worked for companies supplying fittings, engine parts and machine tools. Harland and Wolff built ocean-liners and cargo ships, as well as warships for the Royal Navy.

In the 1920s another Belfast company, Short Brothers, began to make aircraft. They specialised in flying-boats – aircraft that were fitted with floats so that they could take off and land on water. Today, flying-boats are history, but Shorts – now owned by the Canadian aircraft company Bombardier Aerospace – are still major employers in Belfast with a workforce of 6000. They make airframes and components for civil aircraft and missile systems. Shorts also build the

Shorland armoured car body which is fitted onto the chassis of the Land Rover cross-country vehicle. Shorland armoured cars are used extensively by the British and some overseas armies.

Although Harland and Wolff is a smaller company than in its great days, it is still Britain's largest shipyard, repairing ships as well as building them and making rigs and platforms for the offshore oil industry.

The Port of Belfast, downstream from the city, is a major international sea and ferry port used by 20,000 ships every year.

▼ *Belfast city centre at night, photographed from the Lagan Lookout, built at a cost of £14 million. The lights are reflected so well in the river because the new weir restricts the ebb and flow of tidal water. Before the weir was built, the Lagan's mud flats were exposed as the tide receded.*

THE NEW BELFAST

Belfast itself, however, has changed dramatically. Today, it is a city of 350,000 people, and another 200,000 live within 15 kilometres of the city centre. The older shopping streets have been given a facelift, and a string of new developments, Laganside, lines the banks of the Lagan from the city centre to the suburbs. A weir has been built across the river to create a lagoon or lake 2.5 kilometres long and to keep it at a constant level as the tide ebbs and flows. A tower at one end, the Lagan Lookout, enables visitors to view the riverside scene. The Waterfront Centre nearby, opened in 1997, includes a concert hall seating over 2200 people and a 500-seat studio space for smaller productions. Tower cranes are everywhere, building new hotels, office blocks and apartments. After years of neglect, Belfast is building a new future.

THE TITANIC

The most famous ship ever launched from the Harland and Wolff shipyard was one whose first voyage ended in disaster. She was the SS *Titanic*.

On 10 April 1912 the *Titanic* set out on her maiden voyage across the Atlantic to New York. She was the most luxurious ocean-liner afloat and, its owners claimed, unsinkable. There were 2207 passengers and crew on board.

Four days later, at 20 minutes before midnight and with two-thirds of the crossing over, the *Titanic* struck a huge iceberg. Frantic radio messages were sent out, but there was no answer. There were too few lifeboats for everyone on board, and many could not be lowered. The *Titanic* finally sank at 2.20 am on 15 April, two hours and 40 minutes later. Over 1500 people went to the bottom of the Atlantic with her.

Was anyone to blame for the disaster? No one has been able to decide. But the disaster led to new laws on the provision of lifeboats and the introduction of patrols in the North Atlantic during the iceberg season.

▲ *The Titanic on her trials in Belfast Lough in March 1912. The trials were completed on 1 April, and two days later the ship arrived in Southampton for her maiden voyage.*

GLOSSARY

alluvial made up of silt and other material carried along by a river

apartment a home on one floor, built in blocks or groups

cantilever bridge a bridge made of spans or beams that are free at one end but fixed and weighted with a counterbalance at the other

cascade a series of waterfalls over rocks

Celtic a group of languages formerly spoken by some inhabitants of the British Isles and still spoken in parts of Wales, Scotland and Ireland

damask a fabric with a pattern woven into it, often used for tablecloths and curtains

drover a person who led cattle from farms to markets on foot

dyke a bank built to prevent flooding

emigrating moving to another country to live

estuary the wide channel where a river meets the sea

fibre a long thread that can be spun into yarn

fuselage the main body of an aircraft

glacier a sheet of thick, moving ice

glen a deep, narrow valley

granite a hard rock formed from volcanic lava

habitat the natural home of an animal or plant

headwaters streams that are the sources of a river

hydraulic operated by the pressure of a liquid such as water or oil through a pipe

iron ore rock that is heated in a furnace to extract iron

limestone rock built up from the fossilised remains of marine animals and other deposits from the sea

literary to do with books

loom a machine for weaving cloth

microchip a small component that contains the electrical circuits needed to make computers work

migrating species species of birds and animals that spend part of the year in one place and part in another

moraine rocks scraped away by glaciers and left behind when the glaciers move or melt

nutrients chemicals in the soil that are absorbed by the roots of plants

pastureland land on which livestock can feed

pedestrianised open only to people on foot

permeable allowing liquids, especially water, to pass through

rapids a shallow part of a river where the current flows quickly over rocks

reservoir a natural or artificial lake used to store water

rolling-stock passenger and goods vehicles used on railways

sediment ground-down pieces of rock and other material carried along by a river and later deposited on the river banks or bed

silt sediment that has been ground down still further to form mud, clay or sand

source the starting-point of a river

spa a town or city with hot springs in which people bathe to improve their health

suspension bridge a bridge in which the deck is hung from cables

threshing beating corn to separate the grain from the husks

tributary a smaller river that flows into a larger river

watershed the dividing line between the sources of two separate rivers

INDEX